AWAKEN!

A Collection of Poems

Sylvia Sánchez Garza

 Crimson Cardinal Press

Edinburg, Texas

crimsoncardinalpress.com

ISBN-13: 979-8-9884810-4-1

ISBN-ebook: 979-8-9884810-5-8

Library of Congress Control Number: 2024907979

Made in the USA

DEDICATION

*This book is dedicated to my loving parents.
I love and miss you both beyond words.
Thank you for believing in me!*

*IN MEMORIAM
Elida Reyna Sanchez (1933 - 2019)
Joe V. Sanchez (1932 - 2021)*

AWAKEN!

A Collection of Poems

Sylvia Sánchez Garza

Table of Contents

AWAKEN!

A Collection of Poems

Awaken: A Collection of Poems

Awaken!

Awaken!
Your glowing, golden eyes
Illuminate beyond...
Pouring hearts from the rainbows.

Wherever you go
The sun smiles, sprinkling tiny fragments
Oh, the moon smiles back-
Shine on eternal beauty.

Wherever you exist
Your golden eyes glow forever-
Iridescent through eternity Through
the opaque veil...

Sneaking a peek
Of angelic spirits,
Going about their everyday lives
Soaring, spinning, singing their la la la's

As the bead of an iridescent tear
Splashes salt onto the green earth,
And love and life blends into
Chaos and struggles in-between blurred worlds.

In your mind...
The words overflow
Like faucets with broken handles But
from your mouth,

Silence-
Blocked lumps in your throat burn Through
to your stomach.
A bottomless pit extinguishes
But does not crush,

For you know, those precious lost words
Will ignite and explode
In their own time, even if just In
your mind.

Dance

You dance
Flamboyantly-

Rhythm flowing in fury
Buzzing beyond, boundless,

Hostile hands hurling anc heaving
At you.

Adorned in black velvet,
You mingle in the mist with magical eyes,

Perfecting a passionate routine.
SWAT!

Almost-
Had you!

The swatter sits back down
Silently, smirking,

Patiently prepping for battle.
Evade nor escape your epilogue!

Still...
You dance-

Wide-eyes, you shout,
WAIT!

Can't you let us be?
If you had

But three weeks,
Wouldn't you

Dance?
Wouldn't you

Want to spin-in somersaults, to
Dance

Through the steam with your love?
Enjoying your lightening life,

Without worrying about getting smacked
By yesterday's news.

Love squished to nothing.
United.

Unwavering,
We remain.

No need for brutal, violent bloodshed...
We won't go away!

We'll multiply.
Coexist with us

In camaraderie.
Denounce your denial,

And let us-
Dance.

Delusional Dream

Today is a new daily record. Again, we peaked! Still,
does death even care or take pause?
Like a prisoner released from a cell, he
walks in a disturbing, dark daze,
hoping that somehow things won't turn. Oh...
How many more added onto the lethal list to bury?

Please name don't be with the souls we will bury
for we weren't aware that you had peeked.
You had no idea we would be in this monumental mess. You don't owe
your total being. Yes, if only there had been a sooner pause,
maybe we wouldn't be waiting days and days to
stir up a bargain or a deal to sell.

Are any of you willing to sell
your lovely life as blissful as a berry?
Mere bones in a box of whys, in a disillusioned daze-
Still, life mourns as we peak.
Numbers, data, science, they don't pause. The
coaster keeps going, no end, and, oh...

Hospitals become rivers, overflowing. Oh, businesses
may suffer, can't open or sell.
And strangers, with bare faces blaring and barking, raising their paws.
Isn't safety better? Not cremate or bury?
Who cares if the economy hasn't yet peaked
or why the delusional dream is like a devilish daze?

Sylvia Sánchez Garza

Creation walks in mourning, unaware of the darkest days.
Hoping for the promised miracle cure-to us, they owe.
Looking into pandora's box, the world peeks
after being locked away for months in a comfy cell.
Please don't tell us today we have to bury
our dreams and hold on as we all pause

For breath after breath. Respectfully reflecting our reality, time pauses
as we whisper through the window of life and deflect our daze.
At the dreams cemetery, dripping in blood, we won't bury
our souls. We will rise onward as optimistic outliers, oh
with every power in our being, in every cell-
Longing for Love and Peace...our curiosity piques.

Oh, trees and flowers and birds take pause.
The sky is a misty daze in your eyes, bones, and cells.
Try to bury the truth? The sun will cry as we peek.

Labores

los labores lush with life
leaving home, leaving family,
leaving friends, leaving school...
that's how it was for mommy and *papi*
work, work, work thousands
of miles away... *algodon,*
naranjas, tomate llenen los
trokes
sun up to sundown
picking all day long only
to be left behind
when trying to get ahead

Please

Please, no border wall-
No fence, no barrier, no aluminum slats,

For they bleed hate.
Let us be, as we should

Coming and going-
Between two neighboring countries,

Smiling and embracing each other in passing-
Families united,

By an overflowing river
That dances with joyous life,

Not just of splashing water
But of love and respect for one another.

Please, let us continue
Our friendship and unbreakable bond,

Wiping tears never before known
For our blended cultures and traditions

Unique only to us-
To our communities, separate, yet one,

Wrapped in the warmth of our bleeding sun
Desperately trying to stop the hemorrhaging.

Please, don't harm our people,
Especially not our children, for they are innocent souls.

Protect our wildlife, crying dry tears,
Living amongst our destined divide,

For they too share our angelic land.
Please, we are the ones living here.

Let us be, and allow us to leave behind
The bountiful beauty meant for generations to come.

Please, no border wall-
No fence, no barrier, no aluminum slats

For they bleed hate.
Let us be, as we should.

Remember

Is your mother here? She's been gone for days?
Scratching the grey on his head, he lies back-
Comfy in his makeshift hospital space.
I sit down, picking up his paperback,

positioned right next to the oxygen.
The nurse walks in, checking his blood pressure.
You feel all right? And gives him medicine.
Again, he asks... She's not here... I answer.

Remember? She's gone... I haven't seen her.

No??? He says... She was just here yesterday.
Where's your mother? Have you seen my daughter?
Holding his hand in mine- it's me, I say.

Trying to remember my face, unclear-

With watery eyes... I smile. Yes, She's here.

September

It's been a year since my heart broke beyond repair.

Still, the hole soars deep, like a neverending bottomless pit.

I'm freefalling...

Spiraling, spinning, and spinning...

A silver slice of a shattered moon

shooting down to earth with no place to land, out of control.

That September day...a nightmare, I continue to live

over and over in my mind hoping the outcome paints change.

Like a paragraph in a horror novel, I read the same words in a loop, stuck.

Why, my beautiful mommy?

Why? Love- I thought I knew.

Now your unconditional love lingers beyond touch.

My sun spills empty, crying unknown tears.

"Everyone has their set time," you said.

How did you know? How could you have known?

I sit, staring at the endless eternity-

and wonder as I absorb your smile in my mind.

I hear your tender voice in the blazing red cardinal

singing hello at my windowsill.

Oh! As the white Calla Lilies I planted by the patio last spring

dance with you in the wind,

the sun smiles in golden rainbows.

I sense you in my beautiful grandbaby's silky-smooth skin

as she jumps for joy,

wrapping her tiny arms around my neck.

You're in my words as I type everything on my laptop, key after key.

You're in my tears caught in my throat with every magnified memory,

like the dew on a rose's pedal after the break of dawn

slowly rolling off my chin;

joining its fate among the rest...

bouncing off the floor no challenge for the crumpled tissue.

You're in the ceilings and walls of our home,

still holding your floral scent

and in the cracks of the kitchen linoleum floor, tingling my toes.

Why? Sweet, Mommy, why?

Why did it have to be your set time?

Spiritless Stone

Please listen...it was never even my idea to be here.
My marble, resin, plaster, and stone
will someday be gone like my original bone
erased from the face of this bruised and bleeding sphere,

Crying red tears for healing, longing
for forgotten freedom, vanishing in historical hallucinations.
It wasn't my idea to be here. Are you listening?
I am nothing but rock-spiritless stone screaming.

I have no feelings, no emotions-
Pinch me, topple me, break me...
I care not what you do, nor of my irony.
Peace and equality, optimism unspoken?

I'm not meant to illuminate, year after year, standing stoic.
Please...cut me, smash me, destroy me-bloodless and unheroic

Understand

Why look for him in there?

It is but a sacred shell
overflowing with families
and strangers
filling the hard, wooden pews.

Filing in the confessional booth-
falling on knees before a man of white cloth,
reciting and repeating
bead by bead-

Singing sins in melodic,
memorized prayers.
Santa Maria Madre de Dias ruega
por nosotros, pecadores...

Why look for him in there?

He lives inside of you-
inside the depths
of your soul-
where no one else can go.

He's in the atoms and molecules that you
breathe-
the translucent mist in the shape-shifting clouds
that envelope you;
the sparkling water that you drink.

He's in the grass,
in the trees, and in the dancing flowers
that sway in the soft breeze-
brushing past you.

They understand.

29

He's in the simplistic songs about shooting stars- and
in the miraculous sea turtles
crawling towards the crashing ocean-
singing praises as they make their victorious swim.

They understand.

He's in the red, candescent cardinal Perching
on the windowsill
saying good morning
and winking at you,

and in the majestic pelicans
serenading each other
in languages only he understands
as you cluelessly slip by.

They understand.

He's in the breath that goes effortlessly through your body
and through the cells pounding through your purplish, blue veins
giving you goosebumps
and sending chills down your back.

Look deep into the depths of your soul
He is every minute particle of
you, of me, of us-
A sacred shell?

Why look for him in there?

Attack

Attack
with ease...
tigers are sweet
in comparison.

Blocking squinty eyes,
shooting darts that fly
through the mind.
Throwing blood-flavored words

like swords deep into my broken heart.
I know not
how you can be
so vicious?

While I remain-
Silent,
Nada,
throughout the attack.

Wandering, wondering, how...?
In my mind, the words overflow
like faucets with broken handles
but from my mouth-

silence.

Blocked lumps in my throat burn
through to my stomach. A bottomless pit extinguishes me.
But does not crush,
for I know, those precious lost words will

Ignite and come to life
in their own time,
even if just
in my mind.

Anacahuita

You sit decoratively
by the side of mommy and daddy's white frame house.

You were their favorite-
white trumpets blowing melodies in the wind.

Falling to the ground, like gentle snow,
home to the yard's birds and squirrels.

Strong, you stood your ground.
Please, don't freeze; we begged that dreadful February.

For your existence is far more than your beauty.
Your wild olives feed the wildlife around us.

Resist! Survive as you have done for ages,
and continue providing shade and shelter.

Don't you see?
We need you to prevail.

So... Shall we wrap a wool coat around your branches;
white perhaps to match your blooms.

Or perhaps take you indoors
next to the fireplace.

You can relax and sip hot chocolate with us;
perhaps, Popular, the kind Mommy always made.

Sit at the kitchen table and have a bowl of
homemade *caldo de pollo.*

I'm sure that will warm you up
and keep your insides cozy.

35

But don't sit outside in the frigid ice.
Stay with us, *Anacahuita,* and play

your white trumpets
for all to dance in the magical morning.

Stay wild...
Mr. Olive, our *Anacahuita*

Life on the Rio Grande

Home...

an invisible place

where people you love

are forever with you.

Where every experience

shapes who you are

even when separated.

Shared words, beliefs, and foods

yet, two separate worlds.

Caged by a winding snake of overflowing life...

shared cultures, families, and values

yet, forced to choose.

Barricaded by fears of crossing just to see family...

shared work, school, and land

yet, life on the Rio Grande-

guarded, transformed...

Shared stand in unity

yet, hope for opportunity

overflows.

You find each other

again,

and you are

home...

Clouds

Morphing and dancing aimlessly across the sky
mountains transform to billowy sheep,

grazing in gliding pastors listening to the scene below
Wait! I squint my eyes as the sheep disappear-

Now, velvety white kittens are waving hello from above
maturing into grey, dark beings;

always a work in progress,
taking their sweet time.

When the celestial masterpieces unite,
gathering their passion and love,

they pour their heavenly contents
onto the thirsty ground below,

crying tears of joy.
Turning it green and lush,

animals, people, and plants yearn
for rich healthy nourishment.

Suddenly they move aside to
continue their journey of life.

They grow, create themselves
and reunite with each other for strength.

Alone they are unique, but
together they are undeniably powerful,

making their impact and changing the world.
They are the ones

to make a difference.
Unique in shape, size, name, even color,

morphing into the unexpected illusions

Golden

Yes! Drive me up to the sky
where the Golden hues

stand out beyond the rest-
Glorious rays pour everlasting glow below.

Pinks, blues, and greens are simply no match.
Like lucid dreams, we are in no control, but...

Oh! Within the hard empty shell secretly hidden,
lies a miniature hope chest, deep in the core...

Everlasting, eternal peace almost reachable.
Awe! A nuclear force emerging strong.

Enveloping a golden blanket and
abandoning the cold fire.

Explode bright yolk-
forever to be found.

Seeping inception, belonging to you and me.
Now, step forth, sweet, saintly soul.

Take life as your burning crown!
And sing praises evermore.

Haibun
Meditating in the Backyard

I sit on the rusty bench and watch the South Texas Great Egrets settle down for the evening. The summer sun goes down, and cicadas sing in harmony. An iced cold glass of tea in my hand sweats tiny, lucid pearls as I sigh. Where do they go all day, and why do they always come back? One by one, they return to their refuge, a blanket of makeshift snow. Now, they are home where they will rest for the night and wake up tomorrow morning before the squirrels, dogs, or birds. Their flight is spiritual, transcending mankind. I take a sip as the mighty plumage watch and then close their eyes.

Pure, angelic, birds,

majestic at water's edge...

croaking a good night.

Soar With The Angels!

Jury deliberation began today.
What is there to deliberate?

We have all seen the horrific scene play out.
We have all wished we could stop the blue knee

that crushed unremorsefully.
Cries for mama meant nothing

to the monster pinning you down
with no chance for escape.

Mister, we are here.
We hear your yells.

His knee will not choke anymore.
You are free.

We have seen the truth.
As the world awaits...

Our hearts know the empty man in uniform
will meet-his inevitable fate.

Oh! Soar with the angels;
we will never forget.

La Flor

Oh, joy! As the sun first peeks from its pillowy cloud,
pouring glorious golden beams…

La flor, like a mellow kiskadee
perches on a delicate shrub branch absorbing life.

Blooming yellow, shouts, "Good morning!"
Singing, dancing, and swaying in rhythm.

Midday, mysteriously like a magician, transcends orange
in the shattered afternoon, transforms.

Finally, settling on burning crimson,
blood overflowing, mirroring painted skies, screams...

Surrender!
To jealous blades of green below

adorning them in sprinkles
of rebellious red, resisting the evening.

Alas, awaken all! Budding anew.
Mother Nature wipes away her sleep, smiling.

Once again, sharing her eternal beauty
With the world-

Hello, hibiscus! Welcome, yellow bloom!
La flor lives on...

La Luna

Que linda esta la luminosa luna-
bright and alive with a crooked smile.

She cries tears of joy,
showering the heavens with her beams of light.

In the lonely blue night, nothing else shines
while the world sleeps, silently singing wordless lullabies.

Waking the wind from a cosmic dream,
she laughs and invites her to join the melody...

I close my eyes and soar past rainbows of crystal orbs
on the back of a blue heron

harmoniously harvesting moonbeams and stardust,
Igniting the darkness with glowing gemlike sprinkles.

Peering and smirking at la luna linda y luminosa...
she winks at me and secretly cracks her crooked smile.

"Flyback any night!"
she sings in her high-pitched voice.

Wide awake, with a mysterious promise
for the morning, shimmering the sky above.

Ah! *La luna,* illuminate us
with your crooked smile.

Tomorrow night, when the heron arrives,
we'll soar over the heavenly stars and stop by to say hello.

Mr. Sunshine

Alas! Mr. Sunshine, did you take a day off?
Did you decide to sleep in?

Did your dream of vacationing
to the silvery side of the sky finally, happen?

Please, be so, dear illumination.
The cheerful brightness of the early morn...

usually accompanied by songs
of white-throated sparrow and the purple martins

masked under the covers of a soft and comfy comforter and
the golden rays remain,

concealed.
Birds' la la las silenced, squirrels nowhere to be seen.

Perfect!
Today is my turn

to sing my drip, drip, drips
So stay in bed luminescence, relax your radiance and

Allow me to spread my love
in sprinkles and outbursts at my leisure

as I sip my morning coffee, with a decorative smirk.
You see, the fluffy grey sheep can hold on no more.

They must express their emotions
and pour out their sentiments.

For you know what happens if they're held within
We do not want that to happen... oh no!

Sylvia Sánchez Garza

Do not worry about the sweet birds;
their silence is for the betterment of mankind.

It is for a brief moment,
their sacrifice will not go unnoticed

Soon, they'll go back to singing undiscovered melodies and
choruses as the sky paints glittery rainbows.

You will reign again, but give me this moment.
For now-

burst decadent clouds,
display your magnificence for all to behold.

Shatter, erupt and overflow in translucent, tiny wet beads
and show us your glory.

Let Mr. Sunshine sleep in...
at least for a day.

Purple Piñata Pieces

Ah! You hang decoratively on display
swaying under the shade of the mesquite tree.
Your colorful, seven-point star swinging
back and forth, back and forth,

smirking, smiling, spinning on a braided rope
at the crowd below.
Streamers and ribbons join arm in arm,
joyfully dancing in the wind,

awaiting and denying the inescapable demise.
Surrendering solidity to sudden
smashing and dismembering... piece by piece.
Oh! Inevitable destiny-

shredding sins so sweet and subtle
into a million mosaic morsels.
Absolving them to a bittersweet hailstorm-
back and forth, back and forth.

Beating and battering-
reluctant, rebelliousness;
showering sweet saintly dreams.
Pure innocence striking your bursting beauty.

Blindfolded -
turning round and round.
One! Two! Three!
Striking with fierce force.

Shadows crying... mourning you.
Farewell, delicate creation;
sprinkling and illuminating tears in your folds.
Why not be heaven-sent?

Reaching beyond the depths of the depths,
where only the heavenly angels dare descend and ascend,
celestial beings unite to scatter rainbow confetti, professing...
purple *piñata* pieces.

Raspas

Ah! we stopped by a *raspa* stand, and-
were sadly disappointed

like when you wait and wait
at your neighborhood Whataburger

for your order... only to hear,
"Pull up and park, please."

When it finally does come,
it's wrong.

Not what you ordered at all,
not even close.

Our snow cone was not a masterpiece of soft, silky ice.
No! It was an overflowing cup of sharp, jagged rocks.

The plastic spoon strategically stabbed through
was no competition for the frozen chunks.

Not at all what we expected
confusing our taste buds,

crunching between our teeth,
making loud, eerie noises.

Not at all what we remembered.
Now, it seems like a lifetime ago.

The soft snowy treat
melted in our mouths,

mingled with homemade sticky syrups-
sweet cherry, blue coconut, yellow banana

dripping, dripping, dripping, delicious droplets
on our clean, pressed dresses.

What my *Ama Maria* made
remains painted like a work of art in my mind.

Oh! Like a mist evaporating.
Savoring the sweetness solely

in my cotton candy dreams.
Licking my lips for every last drop of life.

Ah! we stopped by a *raspa* stand, and-
were sadly disappointed.

Savila

My cracked terra-cotta pot shakes,
with overflowing green, pointy arms and white veins.

Thorns for protection, yearn to puncture
a stranger's skin with their tiny teeth.

Daddy planted the savila years ago-
seized from his garden

where hummingbirds and cardinals
united to sing praises in awe.

"Scalpel!" shouts the welcome mat by the front door
as I slice the dagger like a surgeon.

Oh! Miraculous slime-like gel ooze onto my palm.
Squeeze out, wonderous ailment.

Slather onto my sick, shattered soul and broken heart
I'm thirsty. Replenish me...

Relieve me!
Heal me!

Words

Storming snickers heckle joyful sadness
play out in my mind like a dress rehearsal.

A broken dam, my words
spillover-

Erupting endless emotions, flowing
freely like an eagle soaring

Towards the celestial sky,
spreading wings majestically.

Still, silence screams...
Words create burning boulders

In my throat,
gushing through my veins, trying to escape,

Lost and lingering beneath my soul
promising songs to sing.

Yes!
They will erupt,

Roaring to ignite and
unveil vivid dreams.

Sweet silence, surrender, and
let my words shine

Pestilent Pest

Isn't traveling
across the globe, exhausting?
"Oh, please!" she says,
sinisterly.

Given a golden key to any city,
she enters her new south Texas homes,
sitting back and getting comfortable,
amidst the pandering palm trees... clearly obscure.

Basking in the glorious Gulf heat, chills prevail.
Attending gatherings, get-togethers, and parties-
never missing one, clasping and clinging to anyone available,
refusing to let go-of her one-sided, love-hate relationships.

Brothers, mothers, neighbors, nanas,
she doesn't care
who she bullies into bonding.
They're nothing-numbers.

She hates wholeheartedly, everyone the same,
Loving and gloating in the limelight,
fighting for the top news spot
like some supernova, day after day.

What a pestilent pest!
Even trolling our kids... Please! NO!
How can our innocent go to school
with you on the loose? They need to be safe!

Won't you see the light
like a saintly sinner repenting?
Still, you smirk,
unsatisfied.

We'll stop you with something yet to be revealed
before you do more harm.
So, don't you worry...
Your time is short.

Soon...
you won't be the top trending tweet,
you'll disappear like your destructive predecessors.
And, we will all be free of your evil rampage.

Please,
you pestilent pest, leave us alone.
Stay away and let us live-
in peace and bare-faced.

Cackling,
she stands up, combing her club-shaped spikes,
then laughs at us all...saying,
"Oh, please!"

La Chancla

Never imagined
That one person

would deprive me
of such a dream.

That one person would have
so much power over me,

like a *chancla*
ready to slam down

on the wooden floor.
Why?

When all I want
is to see my world,

to hold it in my arms
as I stare at its eyes,

while the world smiles
and kisses my cheek.

GLOSSARY

1. Los Labores
   The fieldwork

2. Algodon, naranjas, tomate
   Cotton, oranges, tomato

3. Llenen los trokes
   Fill the trucks

4. Santa Maria Madre de Dios
   ruega por nosotros, pecadores...
   Holy Mary Mother of God
   pray for us sinners...

5. Anacahuita
   Wild olive tree

6. La Flor
   The Flower

7. La Luna
   The Moon

8. Que linda esta la luminosa luna—
   How beautiful is the luminous moon—

9. Raspas
   Snow cones

10. Savila
    Aloe vera

11. Caldo de pollo
    Chicken soup

12. La Chancla
    The Sandal